IT'S NOT YOU... AND IT'S NOT ME

HOW BREAK-UPS REVEAL THE LOVE OF OUR LIFE

CLARE DIMOND

Copyright © 2022 by Clare Dimond

All rights reserved.

No part of this book may be reproduced in any form or by any electronic or mechanical means, including information storage and retrieval systems, without written permission from the author, except for the use of brief quotations in a book review.

❦ Created with Vellum

For my beloved Dad

Professor Stuart John Dimond

30.4.1938 - 16.5.1981

* * *

Your task is not to seek for love but merely to seek and find all the barriers within yourself that you have built against it and embrace them.
Rumi

* * *

For even as love crowns you so shall he crucify you.
Even as he is for your growth so is he for your pruning.
Even as he ascends to your height and caresses your tenderest branches that quiver in the sun,
So shall he descend to your roots and shake them in their clinging to the earth.
Kahlil Gibran

* * *

PART I
INTRODUCTION

'I HAVEN'T MET ANYONE YET'

There is no doubt;
even a rejection can be the shadow of a caress.
José Ortega y Gasset

I met him on Bumble and we had a series of completely unique almost day-long dates before he was leaving for a five week camping trip. He was beyond funny, intelligent, thoughtful, easy to talk to, gorgeous, interesting... We had weeks of lovely messages and conversations back and forth while he was away.

He invited me to visit him on his trip. At first I was reluctant. It was his solo trip. But he said that he would welcome the company.

So I went. And I had a surreally magical time with him. We had long walks and siestas, climbed cliffs, ate fresh figs from the tree, drank coffee in road side cafes, laughed with his friends, shared an apple that he broke in two with his bare hands, looked at the stars, swam naked in rock pools...

It was magical. He was magical. I felt myself falling head over heels in love with him.

On the day of my flight back, he drove me and my haze of adoration, to the airport. My mind was full of the highs of the weekend and excitement about the future.

As we got close to the airport, we started talking about where he lived in the UK.

He said, "I thought I would move when I met someone"...

...then he continued (or at least this is what I heard - there is a big difference, as we will see later)...

"I haven't met anyone yet though."

Screeching brakes, scorching tyre marks, sparks spitting out...

Not the car. The car was fine.

It was my imagined future with him scraping to an emergency stop mid-air, off the edge of the cliff. A hilarious cartoon-style halt. I wasn't laughing though.

"I haven't met anyone yet."

I felt my whole body tense up. My throat closed. My hands were shaking. A mist came down in my mind. He carried on talking, perfectly normally, seemingly oblivious to the ice age that had now descended in the passenger seat.

He chatted away, asked me questions. I replied with monosyllables.

All the time running through my head was an on-going stream of outrage: "He hasn't met anyone yet! Who am I? What does he think I am? I travelled for 2 days and spent a fortune to get to this remote place. What has this trip been then? What have all our dates been? What were all our messages while he was away? An extended one night stand...?"

There was the outrage. And then of course there was the shame. At least two types of shame.

The shame of having assumed that he liked me, that we had something together. The shame of putting myself out there only to be rejected again. The shame that I, as someone who talks about this stuff for a living, should know better. The shame of not being able to make a man I really liked fall in love with me. The shame of not being wanted.

And then there were all those people I had told about my trip to see him. My family. Friends. I even told my hairdresser. (Because of course I had had my hair (and nails) done to go on this rural camping trip). The shame of returning from this trip and having to tell everyone the relationship wasn't at all what I had thought it was.

And then in came the loss. This gorgeous man wasn't mine at all. He was still waiting to meet someone. The past wasn't as I had understood it to be. It was a sudden rewriting of the time I had just spent with him. The rosy future I had imagined for us had suddenly been scrubbed out. Loss of present, past and future.

With all this going on, I was a volcano ready to erupt.

I asked him with a leaden, ominous lightness where did I fit into that 'haven't met anyone yet' statement?

He replied and the first words I heard him say were along the lines of 'This is such early days. We hardly know each other.' The logic and truth of this flew over my head like the planes circling the airport.

I was suffering and in need and what he was saying wasn't enough for me. I didn't want to hear that. I wanted declarations of intention. Of how much he cared about me. But I didn't hear anything like that.

And so I fired out words like bullets from a machine gun. I was talking over his explanations. I couldn't listen. There was too much noise in my head.

The conversation ended and moved on to other things with me still shaking inside. We had a bleak coffee in the airport and then a goodbye.

I sent him a text message. He replied with some words which I read as 'thanks but no thanks'.

And I was left sitting in the departure lounge wondering what the hell had just happened...

THIS BOOK IS FOR ALL OF US

The most fundamental aggression to ourselves, the most fundamental harm we can do to ourselves, is to remain ignorant by not having the courage and the respect to look at ourselves honestly and gently.
Pema Chödrön

What did you experience on reading that first chapter?

Familiarity?

Did it remind you of similar emotional reactions that you have had? Maybe wildly different circumstances but perhaps that outrage, hurt, shame and lostness is familiar to you?

Are you in a relationship in which you experience rejection and disappointment?

Are you running the roller coaster of Match, Bumble etc?

Have you been ignored, not chosen, ghosted, shelved, benched, bread-crumbed, cat-fished, cheated on…?

And has it hurt? Has it knocked the wind out of your sails? Left you feeling hopeless, unloveable, undesired?

Have you given up the whole dating thing perhaps because of how painful it is to have your hopes raised and then dashed?

If that is the case, then this book is for both of us.

Thoughtless?

Or maybe you are thinking, "Well that wasn't necessary for him to say that. He wasn't very kind after you travelled out to see him. Anyone would be hurt."

And yes, that could be right. That was the comfort I received from my lovely family and friends (and hairdresser) on telling them what had happened. And of course, let's be honest, that was the effect desired in the way the story was told. It could have been told in a way that makes him the victim and me the villain but why would I do that…?

The story is not important. What is revealing is that the physical, mental and relational meltdown was way beyond a response to someone (and someone that I told myself I really liked, loved even) simply stating what was true for them. In this book we're going to see how it is always our reaction to words and actions that shows what is really going on for us.

And we're going to see how these reactions make it impossible to have what we really want. I was upset because I wanted him. And yet everything in my behaviour and words was blanking him out. The illogic of this is very revealing.

Importantly, we will see how these visceral reactions are a healing space. And that it is through them and what they reveal that we can simultaneously be open to what other people are saying and doing while being clear about how we want to be treated and spoken to.

He's just not that in to you...?

You might say, 'Well he obviously doesn't like you as much as you like him, Clare'. And that might absolutely be the case.

Where it gets really interesting though, and we will look at this in detail, is that in moments of extreme reaction - deep insecurity, shame, fear, resistance - we are not in reality. We are actually replicating the past.

Do they like us? Do we really like them? Are we good for each other? We don't know at this moment.

Information coming in about ourselves and the other is being distorted by the layers of belief, hurt and trauma that are currently running the show.

We'll look at how investing time, thought, energy, money, attention in someone when they are apparently not choosing us is a play out of old patterns of absence and loss.

And why in those patterns of desperation and lack, neither of us exists as we really are.

Only when we have the capacity to hear what the other actually wants and to respond to that from wholeness and love do we come into reality.

The truth sets all of us free.

Not as bad as what happened to you?

Or you might be comparing your break up or divorce after twenty years with my dates and one weekend and thinking, '

Come on Clare, that's nothing. Don't try to pretend that you know what real hurt feels like'.

The thing is, it is never what is happening that creates the intensity of reaction, it is what it represents subconsciously, the meaning it holds.

This is why we might find ourselves more devastated by a ghosting from a virtual stranger than we are from the end of a decades long friendship. Or alternatively why friendship issues affect us much more than our marriage. Why even the death of a loved one may contain less anguish for us than a rejection. Or why a pet dying can tip us over the edge in a way that nothing else has. The events and experiences that we tell ourselves should seem less consequential or important can create the greatest instability. We'll explore why this is.

Get a grip!

Or maybe you are thinking, *"Jeez she needs to get a grip. It's just a man. It's just a date. Just a weekend. Not even a relationship. Just something that hadn't even really begun. And what's with the whole hair and nails thing for camping? That guy has had a lucky escape"*.

You might be quite right and through this book we'll look at grips and lucky escapes and where they come from.

But, before then, have a think about whether there is any aspect of your life or relationships that has the power to destabilise you in a similar way?

Maybe being disrespected at work, talked over in a meeting, being disagreed with or conned is a powerful trigger?

Have you been devastated by a redundancy or exclusion from something you wanted to be part of?

IT'S NOT YOU... AND IT'S NOT ME

Maybe a certain phrase, or tone or a particular glance from your parents, partner or siblings winds you up?

Maybe it is feeling vulnerable walking into a room of strangers, sitting at a family gathering or inviting someone to spend time with you?

If so then this is a book for you too. Wherever our security and stability is most attached is the place for us to start.

THIS BOOK IS FOR ALL OF US.

Although, on the surface, this book is about dating and break ups, really, it is a book about all relationships and interactions in which we feel vulnerable, in which there is potential for rejection and exclusion.

It is about all the moments when we feel isolated, fearful, anxious, shamed and needy.

And it is about how, ultimately, these moments are the gateway to a profound freedom, stability and love that is beyond our wildest dreams…

I DON'T EXIST

Why are you unhappy?
Because 99.9 percent of everything you think,
and of everything you do, is for yourself—
and there isn't one.
Wei Wu Wei

'I haven't met anyone yet' said the man in the car, when I am sitting next to him, having been 'met' (in many senses of the word…) by him several times over several months.

And that feeling of 'I don't exist…'. 'What even am I…?'.

There is no way around it but the cosmic joke was on me on that trip to the airport.

Because my work is about how our identity is an infinitely layered, continually shifting construct that has no objective truth.

IT'S NOT YOU... AND IT'S NOT ME

Someone else's perception of us is not what we are.

Our perception of our own selves even is not what we are. (If that sounds nonsensical - keep reading, we'll look at it in much more detail).

Everything about how we appear to be changes according to whatever distorting filter is in place in that moment. Nothing is constant.

Nothing, that is, except for the life that animates the body and mind.

Or the intelligence that orchestrates every breath, thought and movement.

Or the field of awareness that gives rise to all experience.

Because this is what we really are. The constant and unchanging. We are infinite and absolute life, intelligence and consciousness.

The truth of us cannot be disrupted or upset. It remains as pure presence.

Any thought that we are something that is separate from that unchanging essence, that we exist independently from that place of infinite peace and intelligence is just that - a thought.

And here's the thing…

…I've written seven books on this. I've run almost a hundred courses. I've broadcast over a thousand podcasts. All on the imperturbable nature of our being.

And now I am hearing a man tell me in so many words, 'Clare, you are not anyone.'

And instead of replying *'Yes. You are absolutely right. I actually don't exist in the way I think I do or you think I do. Isn't it amazing?'*

…instead of that…

…instead of that…

…I am falling apart.

I am very much perturbed.

I am very unpeaceful.

I *am* disrupted.

I am not for one second coming from the unconditional love that I talk about so freely.

And this is where life gets really juicy for us. It is where, if we get still with it, the suffering in our present reality is a gateway to something we could not even have imagined.

Reality is ultimately about healing and how the on-going experience of life reveals what is there to be healed.

To do this means walking the delicate tightrope between spiritual bypass and taking reality at surface value.

In this book, we are looking at how reality is never as it appears to be, our suffering is never in relation to what is going on right now, what looks true is never what is really true.

But this can easily tip into denial. It can become a way that we close off from discomfort and avoid the inner work, protecting our version of what we are, our stories and our position because that looks like how we will survive.

We might find refuge in pushing away the experience or the person through concepts like 'There is no other really', or 'This is just my thinking,' or 'This is all a projection'.

But that is just the equivalent of numbing the feelings through drink, drugs or food.

It is the equivalent of leaping straight back into a relationship to try to regain that high of attention and belonging without seeing what the quest for these things is really about.

Our physical, emotional, psychological and spiritual health requires access to the truth while neither denying our experience nor taking it for more than it really is: a gateway to healing and the sanity that we really are.

It is true that there is no objective 'us' in the way that we appear. And there is no objective 'other'. All of it is a creation of learned conditioning, beliefs and perception. All of it is available to change at any moment.

The truth of those words will eventually set us free. Eventually that truth will align every experience of our existence to the love, peace, potential and intelligence of life itself. Eventually through this we will be more 'us', more expanded, more present, more vital than we could ever imagine.

But not yet.

Not yet for me in that moment in the car. Perhaps not yet for you either.

Because there is suffering.

There is a feeling of needs not being met.

There is shame and insecurity.

There is an increasing sense of separation and distance. A deeper delineation of 'them' and 'me', of victim and villain perhaps.

There is protection and withdrawal.

There is conflict, anger and words being blurted out.

There is fear of losing something that looks like happiness. There is the deep fear that our actual survival is under threat.

And that's OK. It's more than OK. It is the perfection of the design.

Because that suffering is pointing the way to the truth of our existence.

The suffering is pointing the way to our true nature of unconditional love. From the knowing of ourselves as unconditional love, all relationships transform.

And every experience we have, every moment of apparent reality reveals the veils over that truth.

Our spirituality is not a way of ignoring or escaping our relationships — and particularly our suffering in those relationships.

Spirituality IS our relationships. They are where healing takes place and the learned idea of ourselves as separate, vulnerable and lacking is profoundly acknowledged and integrated into the whole of what we are.

Ram Dass said, 'If you think you are enlightened, go spend a week with your family.'

What is your equivalent of that 'week with your family'? What makes you the most vulnerable, insecure and raw.

Rejection? Abandonment? Confrontation? Criticism? Isolation? Responsibility? Indifference? Shame? Loss of control? Attention? Intensity? Sex? Vulnerability? Intimacy? Discrimination? Comparison? Dishonesty? Honesty…?

Whatever it is, this is the place of our freedom. It is the place of our truth. It is the place in which we open up to the parts of us that have been long held at bay.

We turn inwards towards what reality is revealing. We sit in the discomfort. This is the only way.

The suffering is never saying, 'Run. Escape all this.'

It is saying, 'Stay here. Go deeper. Stay present until the truth is revealed.'

Liberation is through profound shifts in the apparent reality of self and other.

This shift of reality is not superficial. It's not just about saying, 'He broke up with me but it's OK because I know this isn't real.'

It is a transformation that takes place deep in the subconscious mind, deep in every cell. It is a shedding of beliefs of separation, unveiling the wholeness and ease of being.

The most powerful place of enlightenment is where there is most to be seen - in other words, in the places where our sense of ourselves as lacking, separate, incomplete, unworthy or invalid is most tenacious.

And what better place for this than a break up…??

THE ENQUIRY

We live in a fantasy world, a world of illusion.
The great task in life is to find reality.
Iris Murdoch

This book is really about a series of shifts.

The shift from the mind lost in the drama of its defence system to simply witnessing it.

The shift from living in the past and the future to living in this moment right now.

The shift from imagining we know what is going on in other people's heads to being so present that we can actually hear them.

The shift from trying to push away all suffering to being fully in our body with the immediacy and actuality of its sensations.

When our suffering is greatest it is because the mind is momentarily lost in beliefs that we, other people and the world are fixed entities.

The way through these delusions is enquiry. It opens up possibility. It brings the mind as close as it can get to reality.

That is why the book is structured around 15 questions, each with the aim of creating a space for these shifts to take place and for the mind and body to settle into reality.

Because reality, after all, is where all the good stuff happens.

QUESTION #1: WHAT IS REALLY TRUE RIGHT NOW?

*We take that which is unreal to be real
and that which is real to be unreal.*
Rupert Spira

Imagine we are an animal out in the wild. We hear a rustling in the long grasses that could be a predator. Ears prick up. Vision focuses and narrows. Sense of smell hones in. Our own movements get very very still. The whole physical, psychological and emotional system is focused on that danger. Everything is trained into discerning what it could be. The freeze itself is safety, creating minimum disturbance that could lead to our detection. It is also a preparation for fight or flight, every sinew available for immediate reaction.

The human being is an animal. It is poised to protect itself. To defend. To freeze. To flee. To fight.

Confusion comes in though when the danger isn't an actual threat to physical survival. It comes when the danger is something else altogether.

The confusion comes when it is our idea of ourselves right now, in the present, our self esteem, our sense of being someone who is loved, respected, special and desired that seems to be in danger.

When the threat seems to be to our future, to the images we had created of what would unfold, the happiness we believed was coming our way.

When it is a threat to our past. Our images of how we have been perceived, of the impact we have had are being destroyed.

When it is a threat to our sense of belonging, access to situations, roles, relationships, a new way of life looks like it is now being revoked.

These threats aren't really about survival. And they aren't really about reality. They are a threat to the learned idea of what we are. The more vulnerable and insecure that learned idea, the more these threats will destabilise.

In fact, it goes much deeper than that.

The more vulnerable and insecure the learned idea of what we are, the more the external world of other people is a *projection* of that instability.

In other words, when we are insecure we are not operating in reality. We are operating in a world in which our insecurity creates dangers.

Literally creates them.

Out of nothing.

We have all experienced this. How when we are low, tired, hormonal, vulnerable or ill, a world of hurt and pain can be

IT'S NOT YOU... AND IT'S NOT ME

triggered by situations, words and actions that we have imagined to be there.

Our deepest vulnerabilities are triggered by what is *projected* to be there and its meaning. Not by what is actually there.

And when this happens, in those moments of projecting and resisting the projection, our whole system, mind, body, attention exits actual reality. It is absolutely focused on the threat. But the threat does not exist 'out there'. The threat is a creation from within us. It is a creation of the vulnerability, the wounds, the trauma, the layers of insecurities.

In other words, all of our attention, our resources, our readiness for fight and flight are honed on something apparently external to us that doesn't really exist in this present moment other than as a layer of hurt within.

So not only are our reactions nothing to do with the person in front of us who seems to be causing them, in these moments, we are in fight or flight *against our own self*. We are resisting our own learned idea of what we are. As David Bohm, the physicist said, "Thought creates a world and says, 'I didn't do it.'"

The faster we flee and the more aggressively we fight the more this projection is held in place.

When we are in identity-survival mode we are blinkered. We are, truth be told, momentarily insane. We are not operating in reality. We are not listening to what is actually being said. We are not present to what the other person really is or what they want.

In that moment, our reactions are about our past. In trying to get something from the people in our present, we are really reacting to people in our past.

The greater the strength of our survival reaction, the greater the desire to fight or flee, the more focused in we are on certain words or gestures, the more we are operating in the past not the present, in a projection not reality. And the more impossible it becomes to get what we are desperately trying to achieve.

The thing is, while we are in the midst of it, there is nothing else, no other perspective, no rationality.

The mind is lost fighting its own creations.

The presence we really are is obscured.

We are an automaton, driven by our inner most insecurity, need and shame. We are a handed-down conditioning of lack, loss and confusion.

And who knows how many generations, how many decades or centuries this conditioning goes back.

This moment right now, the perception of reality and of ourselves, the reactions and the beliefs are the result of a programme playing out.

And although it looks as though there is a 'me' making decisions and choices, saying words, making objective assessments - there isn't one. There is just a programme running.

A button has been pressed on this machine. A switch has been triggered. The subconscious programme springs into action. It is like a long running West End play. The script, the props, the characters, the scenery - everything in place? Right. Lights on. Curtains up. Off we go.

We believe in a self that is at the centre of this, making the choices, saying the words but it is all automatic. There is no doer or chooser. It is software of hurt running within the hardware of the body.

No wonder our relationship patterns repeat themselves.

No wonder we always end up with the same type of people, having the same rows and conflicts, experiencing the same betrayal.

No wonder we find ourselves hearing the same things, saying the same things, doing the same things.

No wonder we have that crushing sense of Groundhog Day, of same old same old.

Let's be really clear now about what is true.

This programme is not me. It is a collection of subconscious beliefs. There is no 'me' deciding what is believed or not. A belief by definition is believed. It is not optional. It is a reality that is acquired, changed or dissolved according to what looks true.

This programme also creates how the other is perceived.

And all of this can change at any moment

I do not exist in that collection of beliefs. Neither does the other.

Hence the title of this book, *'It's not you... and it's not me'*. These programmes of belief and perception are not what we are. The truth of us does not exist there.

Our first question, therefore, on our path to the love of our life is, 'What is really true right now?'

That question can bring the mind back, the body back, the attention back, the resources back, the intelligence, the logic back to reality.

And the suffering is the gateway to this. The greater the suffering, the higher the defences, the more freedom and sanity there is in asking 'What is true?'

What is true does not change with perception. What is true must lie beyond ever changing thought, belief, interpretation and association. With this question, the mind that was lost in the reactions, lost in the past, lost in its pain can now settle, witness, and notice. The lost mind has become sane.

The shift from lost to noticing is the beginning of freedom. It is the place in which the truth of us is revealed.

This liberation, sanity and health is ultimately what all of us are looking for in relationships, in places where they cannot be found. Let's look more at this difference between what we need and what we think we need in the next chapter.

QUESTION #2: WHAT IS REALLY NEEDED?

Wholeness does not mean perfection: it means embracing brokenness as an integral part of life. Knowing this gives me hope that human wholeness - mine, yours, ours - need not be a utopian dream, if we can use devastation as a seedbed for new life.
Parker J. Palmer

In the midst of our suffering, we have a skewed view of what is really needed. And the greater the suffering, the more skewed the need and the more desperate we are to get it.

It looked like I needed the man to make me feel valid and worthy. The only way he could do that would have been by convincing me how much he cared about me, how special I was...

Because then I would feel OK. My self esteem would be intact. My view of the weekend I had just experienced would stay as the rosy time I had filed it as. My future as one half of a couple would unfold as planned. The gateway to the world of romance, sex and adventure that he represented would stay open.

But it is not true that that is what I needed. On the surface, perhaps. At the level of ego and insecurity definitely - but ego and insecurity are not what I am. It is not what any of us are. Trying to fix that in place does no one any favours.

I did not need him to tell me I was special.

I actually needed him to do exactly what he did and tell me he hadn't found the person he was looking for yet.

Because what we need isn't what we think we need.

What we really need are the reactions, words, experiences, people and situations that will mirror, in an apparent external world, the conditioning of insecurity, fear and shame so that it can be seen. So that it can be understood, healed and integrated.

Otherwise, this conditioning remains as an underground dictator, subconsciously creating and controlling all aspects of our reality and reactions to that 'reality'.

Getting what we think we need is a 'mini-reward' (as I call them) that satisfies the subconscious insecurity. It is a bonus payment for the underground dictator that says, 'Keep going. You're on the right track'. It is a momentary relief from the on-going search for security and it maintains the search. In fact, it makes the search more intense because to regain the pleasure of the reward gets harder each time.

The rewards of temporary security, approval and validation are a drug. Not receiving the rewards creates a crashing low that makes the search for the next high all the more desperate.

IT'S NOT YOU... AND IT'S NOT ME

This sets our experience up as: Search. Find a high. Crash. Search more desperate. High not quite so high. Crash even lower. Search even more more desperate...

and on and on....

On that trip to the airport, the suffering kicked in and the need for him to say something nice to me, to make me feel better became more intense.

I didn't hear him say anything that could reassure me in that ever deepening state of insecurity so I closed up.

In the airport lounge, I sent him a text which, on the surface, was an attempt to explain what I was feeling but really it was another desperate plea from an even lower state. The obvious but unspoken 'Say something to make me feel good about myself. PLEASE.'

The needs were becoming more desperate. The lows were getting lower all the time and the highs, by then, were non-existent.

There is no end to this pattern because nothing has changed. When life is lived unconsciously, when the underground dictator rules the show, then suffering just sends us deeper (as it did for me) into the addiction.

The problem is the occasional mini-rewards of validation fool the needy, insecure psyche into thinking that one day the reward will be big enough or permanent enough that we will be complete, peaceful, happy.

From the idea of ourselves as lacking, we crave whatever it is we think will make us stable.

From the idea of ourselves as separate and isolated, we crave security.

And ironically, this stability and security is unconsciously sought in the familiarity of old patterns playing out. If we are used to someone we love not being there, not giving us the attention we crave, it is no surprise that we find ourselves in relationships in which our partner is absent or unavailable.

The subconscious capacity to create a reality that continually replicates what is known is powerful and all-consuming.

It looked like my sense of being, my future, my wholeness could be secured through this man. Those lovely days of dating, his attention, affection and compliments were crack cocaine to a system operating on the belief that being loved by a man was the answer.

And when I believed that was being taken away the system went into free fall. I stopped listening to him. I cut off from him.

And I cut off because I actually, and this is very hard to acknowledge, didn't care about him.

It was not him I cared about. No matter what it looked like to me or how much I extolled his virtues to friends and hairdressers. It wasn't him I cared about. It was me.

If it was him I really cared about, if it was him I had really been dating, I would have listened to him. Really listened to him. Of course I would. I would have wanted for him what he wanted for himself.

This realisation puts all our interactions into perspective. Are we really in love with *them*? Or do we just love how they make us feel?

We won't know until the moment comes to listen to them say something that challenges our ego.

We won't know until they want a future that is different from our vision.

We won't know until they stop supplying the nice feelings of validation we rely on.

If we cannot be present to them in that moment of challenge, if we shut off from them when they are telling us what is true for them and what they really want - the relationship is about our stability and not them.

This sounds harsh but, the truth is, they are simply a prop in our quest to find happiness and security. This is not love. This is fear in action.

They tell us they are going to move to another continent or that they are not happy or that they want something different or they want some space and we believe that the intensity of our suffering, withdrawal or resentment is because we love them.

That's not true.

The stronger the resistance to what they are saying, the more clear it is that aspects of our identity are being challenged.

There is no way round this.

When the man told me something I didn't want to hear, I closed him down. I wasn't getting what I craved from him, so game over.

This puts a very different perspective on the whole weekend. It indicates that I was not falling in love with him.

His words, attention, affection and actions were helping me fall in love with the idea of me.

The experience was securing my sense of being and so all was well. In that euphoric state of 'being someone' it is easy for me to say 'He is wonderful. I love him. I would do anything for him.'

But it is just not true. Because not getting what we need shows the reality. Far from doing anything for him, I can't even listen to what he is saying.

In that moment in the car, he was a drug supplier that had turned up without the goods.

What is more unwelcome than that? What invites more vitriol, violence even, than that?

What use is an empty-handed dealer to me, the addict?

The confusion about who he really is goes way beyond that though.

Let's look at who these people in our lives really are…

QUESTION #3: WHAT DOES THIS PERSON REPRESENT?

There's no such thing as overreacting; it's just that what someone is reacting to may no longer be what's in front of them.
Terrence Real

In the depths of an unwanted break up, if you are anything like me, you might go into over-drive googling 'how to get your ex back'.

But, before we lose ourselves down that rabbit hole of internet advice ('The single TWELVE WORD TEXT you need to send which is GUARANTEED to get him back is REVEALED in this book. Available to you for one day only for JUST £39.99." - believe me, I was so close), it's worth taking some time to consider who it really is we are trying to get back.

Who are we trying to get back?

Because one thing is certain - the person we are trying to get back isn't this person against whom we are reacting so strongly.

It's not the actual real person because we haven't been able to meet that person yet.

Instead, what we have been dealing with all this time is a creation. An image or a concept of someone that is projected from our deepest subconscious conditioning of lack and incompleteness.

When what someone says is devastating, the devastation is *never* because of that person and who they actually are. It is because of what they *represent*. It is because of what they temporarily seemed to secure in us. It is because of what they temporarily held at bay.

In my work, people tell me about suicide attempts after being rejected, about the descent into alcoholism or drug abuse, about months or even years unable to work, sleep or socialise, about deep depression or intense anxiety.

And someone might say, 'Oh for goodness sake. Pull yourself together." But reactions like this are absolutely understandable. They are understandable because they have nothing to do with the present day and everything to do with the trauma, shocks and confrontations of the past.

The intensity of our suffering, our defensiveness, our neediness, our withdrawal, our reversion to child-hood behaviour, our fight or flight reactions is making something clear…

The person we are reacting against in this moment is not the reality of them. In this moment they represent a conglomeration of figures and experiences from our past associated with loss, absence and insecurity. The person in front of us right now is a mirror. He or she is a reflection of the people in the past whose presence, attention, love and approval we craved and couldn't, for whatever reason, access.

These moments of suffering reveal what is really going on. Our emotions and our reactions are revelatory. They are making transparent the layers of loss. Each moment is an accumulation of everything that has gone before.

We think that our devastation after a break up is because of the other.

It never is.

We think the constant monitoring of our phone messages is because of how much we want to hear from them.

It never is.

We think that our anger towards the other and our need for them to feel as sad, lonely and rejected as we do is because we loved them so much and they betrayed our love.

It never is.

True love is not devastated by another person living life in the way that makes sense for them.

The disruption, though, of everything that was projected on to them - the glowing future, the current stability, the feeling of being loved or valued… that can easily be devastated by the earthquake of another person's decisions.

True love does not turn into hatred. It does not even turn into dislike, withdrawal or indifference. It remains as love, perhaps love expressed now in a different form, but love nevertheless.

If we believe the strength of our antipathy towards someone after a break up is a reflection of how much we love them we are fooling ourselves. Love is the same no matter what. Need, instability, fear and insecurity, on the other hand, can quickly become hatred when what is craved is taken away.

My reaction in the car is the visible, present moment end of the chain that invisibly goes back through every unhealed aspect of my psyche. It is the accumulation of every experience that has not yet been reconciled and which is still a subconscious source of pain no matter how fine I might seem on the surface or how much I might blather on about wholeness.

In it, could be, among infinite other shocks to the system, all the unresolved aspects of the divorce from the father of my children, my first boyfriend who dumped me for my best friend, and everyone in between and, of course, my father who died when I was ten.

Who knows what other inherited losses and trauma from previous generations are handed down imprints on our psyche?

That is who we are reacting to in this moment. That is who we are trying to get back. That is what we are looking to put right when we check our phone every two minutes.

And the thing is we can never get *that*. Those people have gone. That moment has gone. The person we were at that time has gone. Even if the characters of the past are still alive, we can never go back to that moment of need and secure what it is we needed.

And so now, here in the present, we remain in limbo. We believe we are living this moment now but really we are still living out the past.

IT'S NOT YOU... AND IT'S NOT ME

You might protest against this. You might say, 'That's got nothing to do with it. I'm fine. I just want to be treated with respect and kindness that's all. I'm just reacting to not being treated kindly. I just want to be valued and supported and loved.'

Of course we want to be treated respectfully and kindly. Of course we want to be valued, supported and loved by the people in our lives.

And we will be. We really will.

But as long as there is that intensity of reaction, as long as we continue to launch into stress responses and survival mode, as long as the armour comes on, as long as there are buttons being pressed, as long as we close down, our freedom can only be found in seeing what is really going on, not in ignoring it.

In these moments, we are reacting to the past and we are not open to the present.

In these moments, there is something else going on that is demanding to be seen and healed.

When it is healed, we will relate to people as they really are.

We will love them unconditionally.

Our needs will relate to the present and will therefore be fulfillable.

We will ask for what we want from freedom and peacefulness.

We will get what we want because it is completely aligned to the lived experience of what we are.

Our partners, friends, bosses, colleagues, family will not be the ghosts of the past carrying bottomless buckets.

When these wounds are healed, it will be abundantly clear that we are wholeness surrounded by kindness and always have been.

We will live in love.

But not yet. Because we are not connected to the present. The past is dictating the reality that surrounds us. It is dictating our words and behaviours. It is dictating how everyone in our life appears.

We only get to meet the real person when we need nothing from them.

We meet them when we don't need them to love us, to affirm us or validate us.

We meet them when they don't represent anything or anyone else.

We meet them when the relationship says nothing about us.

We meet them when we are fully present to them, their desires, their needs.

We meet them when we are healed, when the pain of our past losses and traumas are met with, understood and integrated within our whole.

And when we really meet someone we receive everything we could ever ask for. Everything.

And so, let's get very real with this…

The question, *'How do I get them back?'* is over.

IT'S NOT YOU... AND IT'S NOT ME

It has no relevance. It is not healthy or sane. It contains no actual consideration for the other or for ourselves. No regard for reality or for truth.

We might well get them back (who knows - that TWELVE WORD TEXT might actually work) before what needs to be seen within us is seen. And all that will do is set the hares running and put the hamster in its wheel all over again. It will just kick off another cycle of chase in which the harder we seek, the more out of reach the other becomes, the more firmly our sense of lack embeds.

There is no doubt. The question, 'How do I get them back?' is completely redundant.

Which gives us space now to look at a much bigger, more profound, more liberating question:

'Why is it that the more we want something the further away it gets?'

Let's look at that in the next chapter.

QUESTION #4: WHY IS IT THAT THE MORE WE WANT SOMETHING THE FURTHER AWAY IT GETS?

We'll continue to lose what completes us until we realise we are already complete. That's what pain teaches you— that you'll always have a wound when your wholeness depends on another... and your love will always be conditional when it comes with the condition that you are incomplete without them.
Mark Groves

For all those who believe in it, this is where the laws of attraction and repulsion kick in reliably, every time.

For all others, this is where simple logic plays out, inexorably.

Let's see what is going on.

The more desperately we want or need someone or something, the further away they appear.

IT'S NOT YOU... AND IT'S NOT ME

The more relaxed (sane) we are about having or not having someone or something, the more obvious it is that we have everything we could need already.

Let's go a level deeper with this. Let's look at what is really going on with that desperate want or need.

The need comes from the belief that the person or thing will secure our sense of being, will stabilise us, will push away all negative experiences, will guarantee only positive experiences, will make us complete, worthy and valid.

As we have seen already, the attempt to secure who we think we are through someone that can only, in our confusion, represent our lack and incompleteness is a set up for suffering.

We go after this person as though life depends on it, because it looks like it does. But all that we are going after is a repetition of the same experience of insecurity, the same sense of loss, the same feeling of being rejected or not good enough.

Our interactions with this person, therefore, instead of being complete and real, are just an on-going experience of the very thing we are most trying to avoid. The deeper into this pattern we go the more obvious it is that what we think we want is moving further and further away.

Remember in the previous chapter when we looked at what the person represented? The desperation for the person or thing is only about what they represent. It is not about them. We try to get what we want - security, wholeness, love, peace - through having the person but it doesn't work. The confusion about what is really going on is making security, wholeness, love and peace seem even further away.

The confusion means that the other person will never be enough. They cannot do what we subconsciously want them to do - fix and secure us. This places an impossible burden on their shoulders. Our need is unfulfillable, never-ending and entirely self-focused.

There might be relationships in our lives where nothing is projected onto the other person or object. Where that relationship is enjoyed for just the pure miracle of the other. Where everything about the other is allowed in, rejoiced in. Their needs and wants can be listened to. We might not always agree with them or we might not always do what they want but there is nothing in what they say or do that causes the earthquake of life and death.

In these relationships that are about reality of self and other, we have the whole of them. We have every detail. Every moment. Nothing is pushed away or resisted. This is why in this space of openness and sanity, we have everything. This is the place of true abundance.

It is not the case in the relationships that represent our security. In these relationships and situations, it does not matter how much I think I care about someone, how much I do for them, how attentive I am. When they represent my security and peace, all of this activity is about me and not them. And the proof of this comes in the moment they say or do something that threatens that peace and security. There is no capacity to hold the other. There is no safe presence in which they can say and do what is true for them. Because this is about my survival.

All of this means that my actions towards them are really subconsciously pushing them away. On the surface I think I want them. The reality is I am resisting every aspect of who they are. There is no space for them in this relationship because it is a relationship between me and my unmet needs. While believing I want them, I am actually pushing them away, pushing them out.

Once this becomes clear, it is quite amazing to witness. We can literally see it in action. The relationships which appear the most necessary for our happiness and peace are those that are the least fulfilling. These are the relationships in which we feel we are in a never-ending search.

It doesn't matter whether the relationship is with someone we've been messaging for two days, a spouse of many years, our mother, father, sibling, child, boss…

If that relationship represents our identity, our completeness, the end of our fears, our stability, our future then all our behaviour is actively pushing them away. We are desperate for this security. It looks like it comes in the form of the other person. But the scramble to get the needs met through them means that he or she, the actual person they are, has no real value to us.

It is the same with other things that we think will secure us. Money, our job, our clients, fame, attention, popularity, our body, our health. These cannot do what we want from them and in the process the truth of these things is completely overlooked and pushed away.

Let's take money as an example.

I had a conversation with a client the other day. He desperately (his word) wanted to start a business, get clients and earn money. He felt that if he could do this he would feel that he was contributing to the world, that he had value. I asked about money in his childhood. He told me how his parents used money as an indication of worth. How the first thing they asked him about a job was what it paid. How it was the cause of their arguments and eventual separation. I asked him how much he wanted to earn from his business to begin with. He said, 'I hate money. I don't care how much I earn.'

We can see, can't we, that unresolved state of desire and resistance? I want money and at the same time I hate money. Money is security and at the same time money is instability. We are continually pushing away the very thing we think we want.

Whether this is happening on an energetic level (as the law of attraction would say), an imaginary, dream or non-real level (as non-duality would say) or at the level of interaction and relationship (as psychology would say) doesn't really matter. Because whatever is creating it, this lived experience of unfulfilled desperation cannot be resolved at a surface level. It cannot be resolved with more effort, energy or resources, with better strategies and techniques.

When we live in this surface level of projected reality, all relevant, real and useful information is blocked off. Let's have a look at what is being missed...

QUESTION #5: WHAT IS BEING MISSED?

People will do anything, no matter how absurd, in order to avoid facing their own souls. One does not become enlightened by imagining figures of light, but by making the darkness conscious.
Carl Jung

*Y*ou might say. "Well hang on Clare. It might not be the case that you were projecting on to him. It might just be that over the time with him you did things that put him off you. He might just not like you. After all, you can be quite annoying…"

Believe me, my mind moves easily into over-drive on that front. What did I do wrong? How did I put him off?:

Did I do enough? Did I do too much? Did I talk too much? Maybe I didn't talk enough? Did I snore? Eat with my mouth open? Was it how I looked in the bikini? Was it my clothes? Was I too much? Too little? Too active? Too lazy? Was my hair too styled? Was it not nice enough? Was I too enthusiastic? Not enthusiastic enough? Was I friendly enough with his friends? Was I too friendly? Did I give him too much attention? Not enough attention...? On and on and on and on and on and on and on and on and on and on and on...

This post-rejection analysis (which is always a swing from one side to the opposing other, both looking equally correct depending on the moment) ties the mind up in never-ending knots and has no limit. We wake up in the middle of the night and the mind launches into the interminable back and fore.

It looks like if we think about this hard enough, analyse it enough we will suddenly come up with a break-through answer. "Ah ha! It is this. This is the reason." and then the mind will be peaceful.

But that will never happen.

That will never happen.

It will never happen because there are no answers to be found here. There are no answers because none of this is information from the other person. This is information from a frantically insecure and unrestful mind. It is just a stream of our own conditioning scrabbling around trying to find home. Mental wheels spinning in the mud just create more mud.

It looks like we are remembering the relationship as it actually was. It looks like we are remembering the person as they actually were and what they said as they actually said it. But when we react defensively and close down when they tell us something we don't want to hear, it indicates that we were never really in a relationship with the truth of them.

We were never really listening to what they were really saying all along.

IT'S NOT YOU... AND IT'S NOT ME

There *is* valuable information from the other. When they are telling us what they want, what they hope for, what they dream of, what sort of relationship they are looking for, what they really want and don't want from us, how they are with other people, what they like and don't like: this is information.

This is vital information as we establish whether we are compatible, whether we want similar futures, whether he or she is actually interested in us.

There is also vital information available about how we behave, about the impact of our words and actions on other people, how we are perceived.

But when we are in a relationship with our insecure sense of self more than we are with them, when we pull up the drawbridge, when we get offended, when protection kicks in because what they are saying threatens our dreams and hopes, we miss all of that.

It is ironic isn't it? The more apparently desperate we are for someone, the more this desperation overrides all the vital information they are giving us.

Maybe there are situations and certain people in your life in which you are open and receptive to what the other is saying. Nothing is at stake. No identity is under threat. No survival threatened. Their words can be heard.

With those people and in those moments our whole mind and body is responding in reality, all resources available, all senses open to receive all conscious and subconscious information. Pure presence. This is us, sane and clear. This is the animal of us. A perceptual system unclouded by projection, belief, imagination. Just intelligence in action, in reality.

Me in the car, on the other hand… fighting and fleeing from a threat that didn't exist, ignoring every word that came after the triggering sentence, my voice getting louder, crowding out anything that he could say…

It is easy to see how in that situation, ALL useful, relevant, actual information was being missed. The focus was on surviving an existential threat that had nothing to do with actual reality. The whole mind body system was defending and protecting itself from its own imagination. It was in its own loop of delusion. Nothing was operating in reality.

We do not even know that what we heard is what we heard. We certainly don't know that we interpreted the words in the way they were intended. In fact the greater the emotional reaction the more certain it is that what was heard and interpreted is never what was meant.

Have you experienced that? When there is such insecurity and defensiveness that we lose the connection to reality? When a single word can create a whole imagined interpretation that has nothing to do with what was really going on?

It doesn't matter if it is on a date, with a colleague in a meeting, in a conversation with a child, parent or sibling. It is the same thing.

The defence and protection of the idea of me creates a separation from the other and from reality that shuts off all useful information.

I once had a half hour conversation with a boss and her colleague about my contribution to the team. They began with a criticism of my work and from then on all I heard was criticism after criticism. I became more and more wound up with every passing minute. Afterwards I emailed them both saying I was sorry they had such a terrible impression of me.

They emailed back saying, 'What are you talking about? We're offering you a promotion.'

And this is because the reaction is not about the other person or the current situation or what they seem to be saying. It is not about them. It is about the survival of me.

Or equally, when there is such focus on pleasing the other because of the security they represent, on having their attention or keeping them in the relationship we miss or disregard important information that would have otherwise been very obvious. Signs that this person is not telling us the truth, that what they want is very different to what we are hoping for, that they are not the person for us, that they are not choosing us back are cut out of the picture. In the desperation to have them, a whole parade of red flags can be not just ignored but not even seen.

Which means that this period after a break up cannot be about the other person. These tips and tricks to get them back are of no value because the true person doesn't really exist yet for us.

Our reaction is a sign that there is work to be done and that does not involve the other.

This period must be about us, about me and about you and sitting in the discomfort of our worst fears, our deepest shames, our greatest insecurities and our most driving needs because through that way is freedom.

This does not mean withdrawing from life to lick our wounds and navel gaze. In fact, it is the opposite.

Have a rest, of course, after the shock of a break up or confrontation or rejection. Rest is vital, just as it is after a long run or a serious session in the gym. But rest is not retreat. It is not withdrawal. It is not an exit. It is recovery, creating readiness for the next round.

Rest and then back in we go - for more discomfort if required, more revelations, more healing. We go back into the thick of life simply to open up to what is there to be open to. Staying in conversation to hear what is there to be heard. Meeting our worst fears to see that there is nothing really at stake.

Let's look at how much of this we can take in the next chapter.

QUESTION #6: HOW MUCH DISCOMFORT CAN YOU TAKE?

Our parents, our children, our spouses, and our friends will continue to press every button we have, until we realise what it is that we don't want to know about ourselves, yet. They will point us to our freedom every time.
Byron Katie

How much discomfort can you take?

That's a strange question. Isn't it?

Particularly when we are looking to our relationships - our partner, our friendships, our family, our colleagues and bosses - to *avoid* discomfort.

Discomfort. Suffering. Contraction. Confrontation. Defensiveness. Fear.

It's the opposite, isn't it, of how we think we need to live? Usually our questions are more along the lines of 'How can I stop suffering? How can I be happy? How can I get rid of this anxiety? *How can I get rid of this discomfort?'*

We look to our relationships *for* comfort.

And now, here we are in the middle of a book about relationships considering that discomfort is an excellent thing. Discomfort is the magic place in which everything happens.

We spend our lives seeking out comfort, not realising that comfort is a slow contraction and decline physically, emotionally, psychologically, spiritually.

This is perhaps most obvious when it comes to the physical body.

We understand, don't we, even if we don't admit it to ourselves, that the easy gratification of our sedentary, comfort-eating existence is contracting our world, if not killing us?

We understand that the harder breathing in the gym or on a run is aerobic capacity increasing.

We know that it is the tearing of muscle fibres, along with the associated soreness, which creates greater strength.

We know that it is the ability to sit in the discomfort of cravings that allows habits of smoking, junk food and alcohol to end.

We're not doing this because we are masochists, because we deserve to suffer. We are doing this because we know that staying present, not giving in to the momentary discomfort is where a greater potential is revealed.

In fact the ache, the soreness, the discomfort of exertion and determination start to become welcomed. A positive association with aching muscles develops. The discomfort is appreciated and understood for what it really is - a signifier of transformation, progress and expansion.

But when it comes to our sense of being, the relationship between discomfort, health and expansion is not so obvious.

And this is because when it comes to matters of identity, self-esteem, validity, self-worth and security, discomfort looks like the opposite of expansion and progress. It looks like death.

It looks like any threat to our sense of self will be the end of us. So discomfort is avoided at all costs. And comfort is sought out.

The discomfort of rejection, indifference, lack of attention (or conversely too much attention), disagreement, disapproval cannot be tolerated.

Because that looks like it is the end of us.

The comfort of attention (or anonymity), approval, desire, agreement, validation must be sought out.

Because it looks like that will secure us, turn us into Someone.

And, from this perspective, our life is dictated by the avoidance of anything that will end us and the seeking out of anything that will secure us.

Until along comes a book, perhaps, that says: sitting in a departure lounge in tears is a gift.

Being turned down is a gift.

Being ghosted is a gift.

Being cheated on is a gift.

Being divorced is a gift.

[And this doesn't mean for one second that other people's behaviour is always right or acceptable. Of course not. People's actions can create real harm. The more in reality we are, the more easily and quickly we address behaviour that is not acceptable to us. We'll look at this later.]

It means that every moment of suffering is a gift of revelation.

Before, perhaps for the whole of our lives up to now, discomfort would take us deeper into our patterns and blind reactions. But now it offers the chance literally for a new self to emerge into a new reality.

Our layers of vulnerability are made of fear, shame, need and insecurity. Moments of stress, separation and contraction are when these are triggered.

The learned behaviour in the Western world, at least, at the moment is to avoid these triggers at all cost. To withdraw, resign, block, separate, litigate to prevent these triggers from ever re-occuring. And to numb out the feelings that go with them through whatever means is available to us - food, drink, drugs, sex, scrolling, exercise, gaming...

This way we hope to maintain our mental state, our psychological health, our self-esteem, our sense of being right and valid.

But it actually has the opposite outcome. The attempt to avoid triggering the layers of vulnerability and to numb and distract from all unwelcome emotions and experiences is exactly why we are in the midst of a mental health crisis.

Avoiding, protecting and numbing only ever makes the perceived dangers worse. It shrinks our capacity. It makes us

IT'S NOT YOU... AND IT'S NOT ME

more vulnerable, fearful, shameful, needy and insecure - not less.

Moments in which we notice a shrinking and contraction, a greater sense of separation are the gateway. It is in these moments that we come closer to the reality of ourselves and the other, closer to sanity, not further away.

In all of these moments a powerful healing process can begin, no matter our age, past, behaviour, relationship status or circumstances.

This begins by being still and witnessing what there is to witness. It is attention placed, for the first time on what is real right now rather than the voice in our heads.

As our capacity to experience discomfort expands, so does our capacity to heal. As we heal, the layers of protection that barricaded us off from the world and from our true inner life dissolve.

And the ultimate purpose of this? The reason for remaining in this discomfort?

It is to experience the greatest gift of all: the truth of what we are.

Let's look at this miracle in the next chapter.

QUESTION #7: WHO ARE YOU REALLY?

Deeper than any pattern, deeper than personality, deeper than success or failure, deeper than worth or worthlessness, there is a radiance that is undeniable, always present - the truth of who you are.
Gangaji

This is the heart of the book and why its subtitle is 'How break-ups reveal the love of your life'.

The love of our life is not 'out there'. It is not someone or something that we believe will complete us.

The love of our life is the profound knowing of what we are. It is the alignment of every cell, action, word and relationship to this truth.

Everything we have looked at so far in this book is leading us to the most profound question we could ever ask - who am I?

In fact, everything we have ever done and experienced in our lives is leading to this place of revelation. All our relationships. All events. All conversations. All reactions. All patterns. Language. Labels. Beliefs. Associations. Meanings. All of it has led to this moment of asking right now.

The accumulation of all of this, the on-going layering of belief upon belief, has led to this experience right now of what we are and what the world is. It has also led to all behaviours, reactions and responses.

This is the programme running. This is learned conditioning in action.

And as we saw in chapter #1, there has never been a 'self' deciding what conditioning would be acquired, what beliefs would be believed, what associations would be formed.

In other words, the mind body system is a programme running *without anyone in charge*. There is no central decider within that programme, no matter how much it is believed that is what we are.

This collection of beliefs and reactions, this programme - is that what we are?

How can it be?

First of all, everything that is known about the self and the world is held as beliefs. From the moment of interacting with the world, beliefs have been taking shape. There has never been anyone deciding what would be believed. They have just been automatically acquired by a brain wired to form concepts, categories and rules.

These beliefs were not created by us. And the content of these beliefs does not represent us in anyway.

This takes us to the second inarguable point that these beliefs are not fixed in place. From one moment to the next these beliefs and reactions can shift and disappear completely. (Again there is no 'me' deciding how and when that happens). And importantly, what we are does not disappear or change with them.

There is a constancy to what we are that is way beyond the shifting landscape of beliefs and reactions.

The learned idea of what we are is necessarily based in incompleteness. It is defined through comparison and separation. I am this but not that.

This is taking us to the realisation that, yes, there is a mind body system. This mind body system is programmed by information acquired and believed and the output of this acquisition is all behaviour, words, actions and experiences.

The mind body system and all its experiences does not exist in its own right.

Without the constant, infinite and absolute it is nothing.

Without consciousness, there is no appearance of this system.

Without life, there is nothing animating it, bringing it into existence and form.

Without intelligence, there is nothing governing its operation.

Without beingness, there is no sense of existence.

What are we then?

A programme of transient beliefs automatically acquired with the potential to change at any moment?

Or the intelligence and presence that gives rise to that programme?

This is the fundamental shift.

Believing ourselves to be separate from the whole, believing ourselves to be the programme we are necessarily incomplete. Life is lived unconsciously and its purpose is the search for completeness. As we have seen, this search pushes everything that is needed further and further away. Patterns repeat and create more evidence for the believed idea of self and world.

Understanding ourselves to be what doesn't change, is something else altogether.

It means that life is lived from presence, pure potential. The actions and reactions of the body-mind can be observed. They are now information about what is believed, about the programme running. They are not what we are.

This truth of who we are might be seen clearly in some areas of our life. There might be ease, presence, openness, a sense that separation is not possible.

And there might be other areas in which the experience of what we are is continually thrown back into the programme. Vulnerabilities are triggered, the patterns of protection and defence kick in and our sense of what we really are is momentarily lost. The suffering is great. We are desperate to find home and we cannot find it where we are looking.

In these areas the suffering itself is revealing what is going on. It is showing that there are layers of fear, insecurity, shame and need that are there to be seen, understood and integrated into the wholeness of the system.

And this takes us onto our next question: *How?*

'How can what is there to be healed be healed?

Let's see…

QUESTION #8: WHAT HEALS THE HURT?

Only living stillness, stillness without someone trying to be still, is capable of undoing the conditioning our biological, emotional and psychological nature has undergone. There is no controller, no selector, no personality making choices.
Jean Klein

The unconscious mind seeks peace and happiness in the present, in current relationships and circumstances.

This search for peace, happiness and fulfilment maintains all the layers of hurt. It says 'the solution to my pain, loneliness, sense of lack, insecurity is 'out there' and one day if I try hard enough I will find it.

This is not healing anything.

It is just a life-long attempt to stabilise what cannot be stabilised, to secure what cannot be secured.

Whether conscious or subconscious, the belief is:

If only they loved me then I would be happy.

If he or she committed to me then I wouldn't be anxious any more.

If I could just have a relationship that works then it would make up for my awful childhood and make me whole again.

If I can make sure no one ever shouts at me, controls me, hurts me again, I will be OK.

I can only be peaceful if I know I never have to experience that again.

With this overriding motivation to secure and control we either go out into the world seeking what it is we think we need or we withdraw from the world trying to protect ourselves from what we think we need to avoid.

The mini rewards of their love and attention or the mini reliefs of avoidance of threat are successes in this quest.

But really they are sticking plaster masking a wound that needs air to heal.

The plaster will hide what is really going on for us until something happens.

Perhaps the supply of validation is withdrawn… This could be the result of a break up or the loss of a job, position, role or circumstance that propped up our sense self, of no longer getting the attention or approval we are used to from clients, family, friends.

Or the high of the reward is waning and we need more and more from the other - more commitment, more attention, more adoration - until nothing does the job anymore.

Or we find ourselves unable to continue to hide away and protect ourselves. For whatever reason, we might be compelled to move out into the world.

Either way, it starts to become clear that there is no salvation or peace in trying to secure the present and future. Instead the present is the way to understand, honour and heal the past.

To understand how all our interactions in this moment, especially the most painful, are the space of healing, let's go right back to the beginning.

Conception. The origin of the mind and body that we call us. Life intelligence localised within and orchestrating the development of cells into a form. This form is already being shaped by the conditions within the womb, it is already learning, patterns of behaviour and response are already starting.

Then birth and emergence into a world in which the body is for the first time apparently separate from any other body, while still being wholly dependent on other bodies for its survival.

The baby is already programmed to interact with the bodies, to do what it can to have its needs met. Crying, smiling, looking adorable, eye contact…

The baby is 100% dependent on the people around her. It is not just that she *feels* safe when she is being cared for, when her needs for food, comfort, attention and interaction are being met. She *is* safe. It is the only way that she is safe. And that safety is the only way that her brain can develop in the way it is designed to.

And all the time learning, learning, learning.

At around the age of two or three, the toddler starts to develop a concept of self and the sponge brain is absorbing information all the time, creating beliefs about what that self is, what other people are, what behaviour is safe or dangerous, how to be. This learning is intertwined with actual physical survival. Our beliefs about our self in relation to others are being formed within a context that our life depends on those others.

This conditioning of the mind body system is ongoing. Shocks might come into the system. Trauma. Loss. Disruption. Danger. Confusion. Shame. Isolation. Fear. Unmet needs. All of it embedded subconsciously.

The child is looking to the all-knowing parent, care-giver or teacher to take away the suffering. But these people might well be the cause of it. They might be absent, busy, closed off, indifferent, confused, conflicted, addicted, dead, violent, abusive, angry, depressed, anxious. For whatever reason, the parent might have no capacity to parent in the way the child needs them to parent.

Or they might be the world's greatest parent or care-giver. They might be clear, conscious, deeply caring with immense capacity and they still cannot prevent need, shame, fear and insecurity being learned by the child. Because no one can prevent it. No one is in charge of it.

Yes of course being surrounded by confusion makes confusion more likely but being surrounded by clarity cannot rule it out.

And so these shocks in the system remain. They are not being or cannot be, in that moment, parented away, understood and worked through. The powerful emotions that go with them are not given an outlet. The view of self and world that they create is not being brought into the reality of unlimited potential.

They remain subconsciously as insecurity, need, shame, fear, isolation - unparented, unhealed, unresolved, unintegrated.

From the depths of the subconscious mind, like an unseen film director, these layers of lack run the show. They are an encoded, embodied experience. They create the ongoing lived experience of self and other. They maintain the circumstances in which they were formed even when those circumstances are no longer in place. The lived appearance of what we are and of what other people are is created from within.

When we are not flourishing, when behaviour is causing harm to the self and other, when reactions are about survival, when relationships are full of conflict and defence it is clear that there is something within that is being revealed externally.

These moments are full of pain but they are the gateway to freedom. In times of suffering, reactions return to the child-state in which the true origin of that suffering was formed. Our behaviour is the behaviour of that time. It is understandably and necessarily childish. We want someone to take away the pain. We want to be made to feel better. We are looking for the 'parent'.

Whoever is the present day, apparent source of the pain is now in the role of the parent for us. Because it looks like they have the ability to take the pain away. It doesn't matter whether it is our partner, our ex, our boss, colleague or even our child. When the other person looks to have the capability to make us feel ok, all focus is on getting from them what we think we need.

And obviously it is not them.

This is not about them.

We can't say that enough.

This is not about them.

This is about a brain, a mind, an emotional system and a body that have evolved along the axis of 'I am separate. I am lacking. I am incomplete. I am not worthy.'

It is about the inner child sitting in the driver's seat, spinning the steering wheel into crash after crash in a bid to be noticed and cared for.

And this moment, this moment of intense suffering is where the parenting begins. Not by our actual parents. Of course not. They also, now, have nothing to do with this.

The parenting of these innermost needs, shames, insecurities and fears is now ready to be done *by us*. Only by us. Not by anyone else.

Not by us as we believe ourselves to be. But by the truth of us. The constant, absolute truth.

This is the space of unconditional love, of imperturbable peace, of presence, stillness, responsiveness. This is what we really are. And it is this truth of us that meets the layers of hurt and pain. This absolute openness allows it all, understands it all. Emotions can be felt here. It is the truth of us parenting the untruth until it is seen for what it is.

This parenting begins by going deep into the experience, into the physical sensations. Not into the labels of them, the meaning, the judgement but deep into the actual sensations of the cells, the tissues, the muscles. This is presence. This is reality. This is sanity.

And from there, allowing whatever it is to be felt. Being with it all.

While anchored in the reality of the pure physical sensations, the witnessing presence can observe where the mind goes, the narrative that is created and to see how it is a creation of hurt and lostness.

This shift from a projected reality in which we are existentially dying to actual reality in which nothing is at stake is available every time we are triggered and confronted.

Let's look at this process of healing in the next chapter.

QUESTION #9: WHAT IS THE HEALING PROCESS?

Every part of your brokenness will play a part in your wholeness.
Andrena Sawyer

Healing is an on-going process. It is fair to say that it is a lifetime's work. Whatever appears in reality to challenge us and our stability is a projection from within. Every confrontation therefore is a signal for the conscious mind to shift from lost within the resistance, seeking and resentment to watching it all happen.

Over and over again.

This is the gift of our relationships.

This is the gift of the contraction and the defences going up.

And gradually healing happens.

This is the place of transformation. Wholeness can never be found in getting what we think we want. It lies in healing the layers of trauma that hide the wholeness. So let's look carefully at the stages of this process.

1. Coming back to reality

We weren't in reality before. We weren't interacting with actual real people. We were living a projection. We were trying to secure something that didn't even exist. And all our suffering, the rejections, the break-ups, the confrontations sent us deeper into that never-ending pattern.

Now though, we are starting to consider that the suffering is not a sign to go deeper into the attempt to secure ourselves. It is a sign to go deeper into the body. To actually feel the hurt. To feel the anger and sadness. To feel that sense of desolation. And we can move through the labels of the emotions to the actual physical sensation. These are sensations that we have spent our lives avoiding and now we are able to sit with them, put attention on them.

This attention on the physical, on the right now, brings the whole mind and body into reality. In this moment we are sane. We are present to what really is, not what is projected or imagined to be.

2. The end of 're-traumatising'

When life is lived from the attempt to secure ourselves it is an on-going pattern of re-traumatisation.

We enter relationships and situations as our unhealed state. We are unconscious. We have no idea that everything experienced is a projection of that deep inner sense of lack and incompleteness. Within these projections of rejection, all that can be experienced is rejection. No matter how well a relationship begins or how much potential it seems to have. We are not living the reality of it. We are living the pattern of being not enough.

When rejection happens, which it inevitably will, it becomes another wound, another layer of hurt, another piece of evidence that we are unloveable and unworthy. We don't realise that this confirmation is nothing to do with reality and is only a mirage created from the original wounds at the heart of our psyche.

The man in a car telling me he hasn't met anyone looks real. He looks real and completely independent of me. And because he looks real, because of what he is saying and because of my intense suffering he is taken as evidence that my insecurity is justified.

'See Clare. You can't find someone. There *is* something wrong with you,' goes the narrative, delighting really, in this evidence because ironically there is a woeful security in our identity of lack being confirmed. And as a result this experience re-traumatises an already wounded system.

In this unconscious state, every interaction with the world is re-traumatising. It is the original unhealed wound replaying itself, replicating itself out in the world, projecting itself onto all other people, providing apparently fresh and objective evidence of our beliefs.

And this understanding marks the end of that. This is the end of the mind body system re-traumatising itself.

Now, our suffering is saying - there is more to see here, this is not reality, this is not confirmation of beliefs of inadequacy and worthlessness. This is the undoing of all of that.

IT'S NOT YOU... AND IT'S NOT ME

This man as he appears, the reaction he creates, the intensity of desperation are coming from within. He is not separate, independent or objectively real.

He is you. He is your trauma. He is your losses.

He is ultimately, no matter how much it does not look like it right now, your healing and your peace.

Stay present. Let this be revealed.

3. SUFFERING AS AN INVITATION TO STILLNESS

The discomfort is understood as the invitation to be still and to observe what is happening, to see the child-hood pattern play out, to see what is desperately needed and how it can never be achieved in this projected present.

This stillness to the physical body and its sensations brings us into reality and allows the creations of the mind to be seen for what they really are: an on-going narrative of what we are and what other people are that has nothing to do with truth.

From now on, every time we feel that sense of separation, of me here and them over there, of contraction, tension and isolation, it is a calm, loving hand on the shoulder telling the attention to just be present to what is going on.

We don't know what will come up in this space or what will make sense for us to do. There might be the experience of intense emotions, particularly emotions that we have rarely felt or which we have pushed away or which we were never allowed to express growing up. There might be lots of crying. It might feel like a storm is ripping through us.

There might be the move to be physical or there might be the inclination to talk with someone who will hold that space for us, perhaps a trusted friend or a therapist. We might find ourselves visiting past places or listening to particular music. We might find ourselves writing (as I did with this book) or creating something.

We don't know. But go with it. As long as there is openness to the sensations of the body, this is not distraction or numbing. It is the expression and release of what is deep within.

This is the heart of healing. It is the truth of us, of what we really are, parenting that small child. And it is that small child moving out of the driving seat and taking her place now in the back seat of the car—safe, allowed, understood and no longer running the show.

4. Re-entering the world to be destroyed not to be completed

The final stage of healing represents a completely fresh way of navigating life.

It has become clear that this insecure version of ourselves can never be made secure. Peace and happiness can never be found in the desperate attempt to fix in place, control or avoid people and situations.

It has become clear that, in moments of suffering, how the world appears and how I appear are projections from within, layers of belief, subconscious wounds turned into an apparent external reality.

It has become clear that instead of life being an attempt to secure this insecure idea of ourselves, everything in life is aiding its dissolution. The entire way reality appears is saying, 'You are not separate. You are not isolated from the whole.'

And so we engage with life to be destroyed. Well, for the idea of ourselves to be destroyed. We engage for every reaction to reveal what is being clung to. This is why author and teacher Byron Katie encourages people to turn their worst fears into sentences that begin with: "I look forward to…"

"I look forward to being rejected."

"I look forward to being let down."

"I look forward to being excluded."

As intense as the suffering might be in these moments, it is pointing the way to freedom.

And it is pointing the way to a relationship, perhaps for the first time in our lives, with the person in front of us.

* * *

THE TRULY WONDERFUL part of healing is that the people in our lives are delivered back to us. I don't mean that breakups turn back into relationships and divorces turn back into marriages - although they might. I mean that regardless of the form now of the relationship, even if we never see the other again, they are now available to us. The thought of them is peaceful and real. They are welcome in our mental life, in our mind and memories. And if they are present in our actual life we can allow every detail of them in.

Let's look at this a bit more in the next chapter.

QUESTION #10: WHO ARE THEY REALLY?

Van Gogh didn't say: "That's just an old chair." He looked, and looked. He sensed the Beingness of the chair. Then he sat in front of the canvas and took up the brush...
Eckhart Tolle

Finally…

finally…

…we get to meet the other person. Well, as close as possible as it is to meet them.

The perception of them still belongs to us, the perceiver.

But with less and less projection of the innermost needs and insecurities onto them, there is now nothing pushing them away.

With less and less meaning of who they are, there are no barriers between us.

With less and less depending on their responses and feelings about us, their words can actually be heard.

The projection is falling away and it is revealing... what...?

It is revealing that they are the same as us.

A miracle.

A miracle of universal intelligence in a temporary, perception created form.

A miracle of consciousness in which everything appears.

A miracle of beingness.

A miracle of life animating a programme of conditioned beliefs, preferences and behaviours.

A miracle, ultimately of unconditional love.

From the space of unconditional love, where nothing has to be secured or changed, anything is possible.

What happens now?

Who knows?

It is impossible to tell. As wounds are healed, the conditioned programme changes and the lived experience of what we are transforms. Desires shift. Attractions change. The form of relationships evolves. Behaviours can be completely different.

The difference is that there is no longer a programme of yearning locked into the other. The unconscious dependence on what they represent, how they make us feel, what they secure or what undesirable experiences they appear to hold at bay is dissolving.

We have become a different person in a different reality —or rather there is a new mind-body programme operating from a more real, whole and complete basis.

It is remarkable how changes happen automatically and almost imperceptibly from this place.

That person who we were so desperate to get back might now simply fade from our mind and our life.

Or we might find them doing what we had prayed they would—calling us, apologising, asking to meet, to have us back—but now something has changed. We can't quite describe what happened but there is just no longer that need for them.

Or we might find the relationship which was once full of angst and heaviness, lightening, becoming fun and easy.

The other person might seem different while still the same. The aspects of their character that used to drive us mad with frustration might no longer even exist. We might notice new strengths and capacity in them. They might even look different to us now.

Let's have a look at this process in terms of the evolution of relationships:

1. Unconscious

In the most unhealthy relationships, two individuals both operating from a deep programme of lack, make each other ever more vulnerable and lost. We are locked in together like two fighting stags, antlers entangled, dragging each other to an exhausted collapse. The roller coaster of control and chaos, validation and vitriol, approval and rejection keeps us both in a state of utter confusion.

Violence, substance abuse, emotional detachment, authoritarianism, absence, blame, self-blame, financial, sexual and emotional abuse can occur as we exacerbate each other's instability while simultaneously trying to escape our own.

It looks like the only solution is to try to make the other change. This can never work.

The only possibility is to see how this relationship is revealing everything that we are trying to escape within us. This is not easy as we are already so low and defeated. To stay present and accountable without sliding into an identity of failure may take everything we have. But it is possible. There are many people who have trodden this path ahead of us, making it clearer all the time.

In reading this book, we have already opened up to this possibility. We are ready.

2. HEALING HEALTHILY TOGETHER

From the moment there is a glimpse of the pattern that is triggered when we feel insecure, fearful, ashamed or needy, a gateway opens. There will be bumps along the road of course. If you are anything like me you might be thrown back into the patterns frequently but there is now a new sense that these patterns are not what we are. Rather they are pointing the way to a deeper existence beneath the transient reactions.

This knowing makes us compatible with people who are similarly healing. It becomes more possible to hold a non-reactive space for the other in their times of need and they can do the same for us. There is open communication about fears and vulnerabilities. There is ownership, apologies and genuine forgiveness and understanding when the mist descends and behaviour reverts.

Instead of two deeply unconscious people dragging each other underwater, two increasingly conscious people are lifting each other up. There is a tremendous beauty in this process. Savour every second of it.

3. Fully conscious

Many excellent spiritual teachers are in relationships that shine with love and laughter. Their partner is often present at retreats and talks and, at the same time, distinct in their own right. The sense of connection, joy and freedom between them is palpable.

The ultimately healthy relationship is between two people who understand who they are at the core of their being. These are people whose spirituality has taken them deeper into life, deeper into relationships, deeper into their true nature. Their lives have been a journey of continually dissolving the layers of lack and separation that would stand between them and any other.

They meet now as truth - unconditional love, peace, intelligence, life - in miracle form. And there is still choosing, preferences, attraction. The form of the body does not disappear because the sense of being has lightened.

It seems to me that this is the ultimate purpose of our lives. For our suffering to be the means of our enlightenment and through that to allow us to see people as they really are. To relate to all others from love and freedom.

We love the other because we are love. We understand them because we, finally, understand who we are. We need nothing from them that they cannot actually provide. We want for them what makes them flourish and sparkle physically, mentally and spiritually. We want to hear their authentic truth.

They are love. They are us.

We are love.

QUESTION #11: WHAT DO YOU WANT?

Desire is an insubstantial shadow.
But turn desire inward, towards spiritual treasure, then it yields substantial results.
Sri Sathya Sai Baba

What we have described in this book is an entirely new way of orientating through life.

The attempt to secure ourselves as a separate entity, loved, approved of, respected and included is seen for the unfulfillable quest it really is.

Now the orientation is towards whatever reveals that separate entity as untrue.

Resistance is a signal to stay present rather than to fight or flee.

Resentment is an invitation to stillness rather than be lost in the endless loop of defence.

Closing down and conflict are signs to notice what is at stake and that they are response to something deeper than what is going on right now.

When we have navigated our lives though through seeking, resistance and resentment, the fear is that staying present to it rather than acting from it will make us a doormat.

It looks like the end of seeking will mean missing out on all the great things of life - the relationship, career, bank balance, health, social life of our dreams.

It looks like the end of resistance will mean we become passive or static, stuck with whatever it is we most don't want, that no change will ever happen.

When we have ricocheted from outrage to outrage, it looks like the end of resentment will mean no boundaries, no self respect.

To live fully we do not need seeking, resistance and resentment. In fact, as long as we follow these three false guides blindly, the true fullness of our life is continually veiled.

In this new orientation what we really want becomes clearer and clearer. Old habits of people-pleasing, manipulation, sulking, control, passivity, aggression and victim start to be seen for what they really are - attempts to secure ourselves. All of these reactive ways of being and behaving covered up what we really want for ourselves, our lives and for other people.

Now though, we are in a new era of transparency, healing and actual information and for the first time, perhaps in our entire lives, we start to receive what we really want.

It comes in the shift from need to want.

IT'S NOT YOU... AND IT'S NOT ME

There are certain absolute requirements for survival. Oxygen. Sunlight. Shelter. Water. Food.

Beyond these, we start to enter the zone in which need and want are blurred and in which (as we saw in Chapter 4) the more something seems to be needed the less able we are to receive it.

Research consistently shows that friendships, loving partnerships and positive interactions are powerful for longevity and health. When these are craved, though, to stabilise our sense of self, the harder it is to establish them.

Living from insecurity and sense of lack turns everything into need, makes it into a survival issue when it is not.

Using the suffering and discomfort to open up to these layers and in the process heal them, means that we come back to reality. This is not life and death. We don't need that person. We don't need their love, attention or presence. And as need falls away, we can receive them.

We *need* to become sane, to heal, and from there we can ask for what we *want*.

And what we want becomes increasingly clear. When there is no sense of self to prop up, no blind desperation - things are much simpler.

We are turning our attention to the real world now, to the world of relationships and interactions, to what makes a relationship worthy of its name and what disqualifies it.

In this real world, we start to receive everything we could ever want. Let's look at where that transformation begins.

QUESTION #12: WHERE DOES CHANGE BEGIN?

We think that we resist certain states because they are there, but actually they are there because we resist them.
Adyashanti

In the aftermath of a break-up or in the midst of conflict, all of our attention is on the separation between them and us.

When we are knocked by something, when we are hurt and stranded and lost, we are scrabbling to regain our sense of self. This self that we are trying to regain is made of the stories of our existence, of the old narrative, of our deepest shame, need and insecurity, of what we project onto other people.

This is the ultimate irony. We are trying to stabilise our sense of being by building up something that is inherently unstable. We are desperately seeking security in the ultimate insecurity of believed separation.

We try to stabilise ourselves by blaming the other. They should be more abc. If they were less xyz then everything would be different.

But all that does is continue to fix the other in place as a concept. To break the deadlock we need to begin in the last place, in this period of pain and hurt, that we want to look…

Within ourselves.

Change begins with us. After all, the appearance and meaning of everything begins and ends with our perception of it. We are the source of everything.

Everything that we want from apparent others, from the world, all the ways we want things to change - it has to begin with our behaviour, our words, our way of being.

It is so easy to stay put, marinading in resentment, listing to our friends all the reasons why we are a victim in any given relationship or circumstance.

But the only way out is to behave in the way we want others to. We have to show the way first.

If we want honesty - be honest. And that means the end of every pretence, manipulation, people pleasing action and lie. It is amazing how dishonest we really are.

If we want someone's loving presence and attention, notice how much of our attention we give them and what is really contained in that attention. We might not actually be as loving or attentive as we like to think we are.

If we want respect - be respectful. In every way, in our words, beliefs, thoughts and actions - to the person we want to change, and all others.

If we want commitment, consider what commitment we offer the other. Is it really commitment to them or rather a commitment to the good feelings or experiences they provide?

Let's forget asking anything of anyone until we have first shown how that change is possible in ourselves.

This does three things:

i) REALISM

it makes it clear how difficult it is to do what we are asking of someone else. Changing patterns, reactions and responses is not easy.

ii) SAMENESS

it shows that our behaviour is the same as theirs - there really is no difference between us and them.

iii) COMPASSION

it brings compassion and understanding, breaking the deadlock of resistance and resentment so possibility and reality can enter.

* * *

THE OTHER PERSON is a mirror of us.

To change other people, the aspect of ourselves which creates them has to change.

There is no other way.

QUESTION #13: HOW DO WE GET WHAT WE WANT?

Someday, after mastering the winds, the waves, the tides and gravity, we shall harness the energies of love, and then, for a second time in the history of the world, man will have discovered fire.
Pierre Teilhard de Chardin

In the taxi once on the way to a party I asked my fiancé at the time, 'Is this outfit a bit too much do you think?'

It was a glitter dress. We were going to a pub.

'Probably' he said.

I didn't talk to him for the rest of the night.

Yes. I know.

In the taxi I sure as hell didn't want his actual opinion. I didn't want what I had actually asked for.

The honest request would have been, 'I'm feeling insecure about this outfit. Please say something, anything to reassure me. And if you can't find something truthful to say then please lie.'

If I'd asked for that, I might well have received it. Instead, I got what I asked for which was the opposite of what I was really asking for and it sent me deeper into a sulk of insecurity.

Is what we are asking for really what we want? In our courses, we call this a 'Clean Ask'. Or is it code for something else?

When life is a projection of hurt, what we ask for is never what we really want. We might ask for help in the kitchen but we are really asking for love. When we don't get the help (remember how confusion pushes everything we think we want away) it looks like we are being refused love instead of just help wiping a sink. No wonder we react with such intensity to crumbs on the counter.

With transparency, honesty and accountability we can voice our inner needs. I want to feel loved. I want to feel secure. I want to feel valid. And voicing these needs makes it clear that these cannot be met by anything in the world of people, actions and objects. Instead the desire turns inwards, is parented inwards.

And from there we can ask for a hug, a kiss, a phone call, a date, a conversation, a marriage, a clean kitchen for exactly what it is. People can give us what we ask for because we are asking for what we want.

The key to a 'clean ask' is that it allows for whatever answer the other gives. Instead of their answer creating resentment and resistance, it is understood for what it is: information

We can ask for anything. The answer might be no. And that is information which allows for ever greater realism.

Will you be faithful to me? Will you promise to be home by 5 every night? Do you want children with me? Do you love me? Do you choose me?

The answer might be no.

And it might be a no that causes us to stagger backwards as everything that we clung to is shaken. But this suffering now is telling us to stay in reality. Feel the devastation in every cell of the body. This is sanity now. Their words are information.

Their words create the space for conversation and ultimately the owning of our own compromises and choices.

Instead of resentment that someone isn't changing, we recognise that this is now on us. We have the information. What we do with it now is up to us.

Expectations turn into agreements or a different arrangement altogether. The compromises we are making become more and more visible. Actions and words that are going against our deepest truth make less and less sense.

The greatest freedom is the realisation that everything we don't want in our life, everything we most resist is an ongoing active choice to keep it in place. It is on us. No one else.

From our identity as wronged and mis-treated this is almost impossible to acknowledge. It looks like victim-blaming. But as we heal, we edge closer to seeing how all reality of self, world and other is held in place through our behaviours and perceptions. The world changes as we move with curiosity about what is actually true.

This way, the layers are dissolved to reveal the relationship, the job, the friendships of our dreams.

Where do we go from here…? Let's look at this in our next chapter.

QUESTION #14: HOW DO WE KEEP EVOLVING?

The doors to the world of the wild Self are few but precious. If you have a deep scar, that is a door, if you have an old, old story, that is a door. If you love the sky and the water so much you almost cannot bear it, that is a door. If you yearn for a deeper life, a full life, a sane life, that is a door.
Clarissa Pinkola Estés

This is a book about the true gift that hurt represents. Let's see how this can be the navigation for the rest of our lives.

1. CONTINUE TO SETTLE BACK TO REALITY

As we have seen, not living in reality is exhausting. It is deep on-going suffering. It is eternal struggle.

When we live in reality, not in projection, we are sane. We want to be sane. Above all, we want to be sane. This is the sole (soul?) purpose of our lives.

It means responding to what is actually going on not what our fears and insecurities are creating.

It means having relationships with the actual people in our lives not with shadows from the past.

Reality is what our minds and bodies are designed for. This is why mental suffering is a sign to bring us back to reality as clearly as physical pain is a sign to remove our hand from the hot plate or the nettle bed.

We exist really (really, really, really) well in reality.

And moment by moment, suffering by suffering, confrontation by confrontation, the absolute sanity of what we are is being revealed.

2. CONTINUE TO LEARN

When it looks like our security is to be found in the presence, approval or attention of the other, we are living in projection. Real life, real time information isn't even accessible, let alone taken into account. We do things all the while resenting the other. We fight and flee. We calculate, pretend and manipulate. We live in a static world of belief devoid of fresh information. We have to. We believe our survival depends on it.

But the body-mind is a continual learning system. It thrives, flourishes, grows, operates and finds equilibrium through direct information and feedback.

When we are sane, we can ask for and receive actual information. People tell us what they want and honest open discussions can be had.

What they want might be an easy change for us, something that we are more than happy to provide now that we know. They might want a bit more help or less help. They might want some quiet for a moment or for us to talk to them. Information.

Or they might want something that is hard, perhaps very challenging, for us to provide but which we know deep in our hearts is healthy for us to do. They might want more time to themselves. They might want us to take better care of our health. They might want us to tackle our addictions. Information.

Or they might want something that goes against our own values or our own health. They might want us to join them in their unhealthy habits or to embark on risky or dishonest practices. We might want monogamy but they might want to see other people while still dating us. Again, information.

This is all information that gets completely confused when we are confused. When it looks like our wholeness depends on that person, we abandon ourselves and our health, information is disregarded and distorted.

When we are in reality, we are sane and when we are sane we can remain connected to the other and to the deepest peace at the heart of our being, whatever they are saying.

It is from this place that we learn about ourselves. It is where our most authentic yes and no emerges. It is where our behaviour aligns to health and possibility. It is where our true boundaries are found and where we find the people with whom we are most compatible.

And all the while, information is sanely, usefully, accountably guiding all our decisions and behaviour.

. . .

3. CONTINUE TO HEAL

Is this job of healing ever done? Who cares. It really doesn't matter. Because now there is excitement about what our resistance to reality will reveal. Every situation can now be approached with curiosity and openness.

We can start going on dates again. We can invite potential friends for a coffee. We can put ourselves up for a new job or promotion. We can contact potential clients. We can have the difficult conversation with our spouse, parents or children. What will these experiences reveal? Will they be reflections of the lightness and unconditional love of our being? Or will there be resistance and hurt?

The lived experience of wholeness?

Or the healing of the layers that hide it?

Either way, we win.

*　*　*

THE ULTIMATE PURPOSE of living in reality, continuing to learn and heal is to, as Rumi said, embrace the barriers against love within us, to understand them so deeply that they become part of the love that we are. In our final question we look at how we live in love.

QUESTION #15: HOW DO WE LIVE IN LOVE?

Lovers don't finally meet somewhere.
They're in each other all along.
Rumi

Ultimately, of course, we want to live in harmony, in love and absolute connection with the people in our life. Of course we do.

We tried one way to get there and it didn't work. It pushed people away. It created conflict. It tried to fix in place people who didn't want us. It lied and sulked. It rode over our deepest values.

Now we know the route to what we really want. We know that these loving relationships are created within us. They emerge to the degree that our conditioning of lack and separation dissolves.

This is the standard we hold for ourselves now. To allow resistance and resentment towards the other to have its true purpose - revealing the unconditional love at the heart of our being.

The intensity of reaction the other apparently creates is because of us, not them. And that intensity is our route to presence.

Unconditional love does not mean always saying yes to whatever people ask of us. Unconditional love is never passive, never a doormat, never does what is not loving to self and other. It means standing in the truth of our being, relating to the truth of the other and in that space, giving our most authentic yes or no.

As Byron Katie said, 'Every no I say is a yes to myself. It feels right to me. People don't have to guess what I want or don't want, and I don't need to pretend.'

The yes or no is entirely owned by us. There is no resentment towards the other for asking. There is no resistance. We are free in our absolute integrity.

Our wholeness makes deep intimacy possible in every moment. In fact it is the foundational requirement.

All actions and all relationships can be an attempt to secure ourselves and while this continues the lived experience is of continued insecurity.

Through healing, through recognising insecurity for what it is, all actions and relationships start to become the most natural joyful expression of wholeness in miracle human form.

The dissolution of separation means that people are safe with us now in a way they never were before. We listen. We hear them. We respond. We are honest. We tell them what we want. We respect them. We love them.

And because nothing is dependent on their loving us back, because they are loved, because there is no condition on their being, because they are absolutely free to not love us…

…they love us.

CONCLUSION

The sculpture is already complete within the marble block, before I start my work. It is already there, I just have to chisel away the superfluous material.
Michelangelo

This is not an internet quick fix.

It is not a way to secure the undying love and commitment of the person who we think will make everything OK.

It is not a way to never feel rejected, lonely, sad or isolated.

It is not a way to get them back or to change their minds.

It is an orientation of healing and expansion for the rest of our life.

It is meeting each moment of suffering in its fullness, of seeing what it reveals and how it points the way to something that is far beyond the wavering changes of moment to moment experience.

This is the end of us as we have always believed ourselves to be.

It is the end of our stories, even the innermost, and the start of living in truth.

It is the end of us as victim or as villain and the beginning of simply asking, peacefully, for what we really want.

It is the end of every element of protection and defence, every place of refuge and the start of genuine intimacy.

It will take courage.

It demands a great deal to be still, to remain open when every inclination is to hide away or to stride out armour on, fists high. But those are the patterns of the child. Innocent and completely understandable. And we are not that small child.

We are no longer helpless in front of the overwhelming, confused in front of the unfathomable, terrified in front of the unknown. We are presence, intelligence and life itself.

Thank you rejection. Thank you loss. Thank you hurt and pain.

You burn through the layers to reveal unconditional love, holding the child gently in its arms, close in, safe now.

Imperturbable peace in vulnerable form.

Free to be rejected, to lose, to be hurt again and again.

Free to continue to love and to heal.

Complete and whole.

This is the love of our life.

Printed in Great Britain
by Amazon